WELCOME TO IRELAND

COUNTRIES OF THE WORLD

Ireland

by Monika Davies

BLASTOFF! READERS 2

BELLWETHER MEDIA • MINNEAPOLIS, MN

Blastoff! Readers are carefully developed by literacy experts to build reading stamina and move students toward fluency by combining standards-based content with developmentally appropriate text.

Level 1 provides the most support through repetition of high-frequency words, light text, predictable sentence patterns, and strong visual support.

Level 2 offers early readers a bit more challenge through varied sentences, increased text load, and text-supportive special features.

Level 3 advances early-fluent readers toward fluency through increased text load, less reliance on photos, advancing concepts, longer sentences, and more complex special features.

★ **Blastoff! Universe**

Reading Level — Grade K → Grades 1–3 → Grade 4

This edition first published in 2023 by Bellwether Media, Inc.

No part of this publication may be reproduced in whole or in part without written permission of the publisher. For information regarding permission, write to Bellwether Media, Inc., Attention: Permissions Department, 6012 Blue Circle Drive, Minnetonka, MN 55343.

Library of Congress Cataloging-in-Publication Data

Names: Davies, Monika, author.
Title: Ireland / by Monika Davies.
Description: Minneapolis, MN : Bellwether Media, Inc., 2023. | Series: Blastoff! Readers : countries of the world | Includes bibliographical references and index. | Audience: Ages 5-8 | Audience: Grades 2-3 | Summary: "Relevant images match informative text in this introduction to Ireland. Intended for students in kindergarten through third grade"– Provided by publisher.
Identifiers: LCCN 2022044143 (print) | LCCN 2022044144 (ebook) | ISBN 9798886871326 (library binding) | ISBN 9798886872583 (ebook)
Subjects: LCSH: Ireland–Juvenile literature.
Classification: LCC DA906 .D38 2023 (print) | LCC DA906 (ebook) | DDC 941.7-dc23/eng/20220913
LC record available at https://lccn.loc.gov/2022044143
LC ebook record available at https://lccn.loc.gov/2022044144

Text copyright © 2023 by Bellwether Media, Inc. BLASTOFF! READERS and associated logos are trademarks and/or registered trademarks of Bellwether Media, Inc.

Editor: Elizabeth Neuenfeldt   Designer: Gabriel Hilger

Printed in the United States of America, North Mankato, MN.

Table of Contents

All About Ireland	4
Land and Animals	6
Life in Ireland	12
Ireland Facts	20
Glossary	22
To Learn More	23
Index	24

All About Ireland

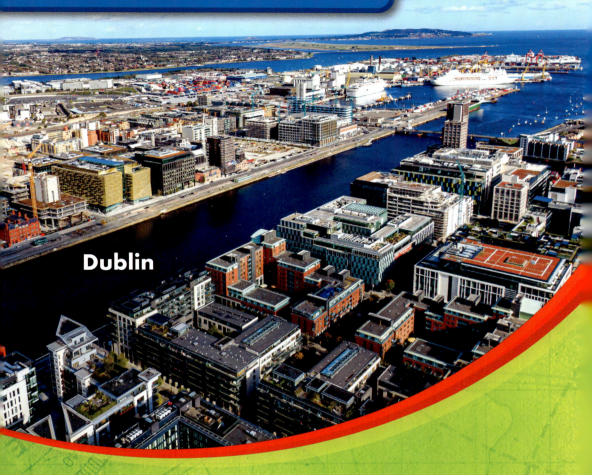

Dublin

Ireland is an island country.
It is in western Europe.
Its capital is Dublin.

Ireland has many green fields. It is often called the "Emerald Isle!"

Land and Animals

Plains cover most of central Ireland. Lakes and **bogs** also cover the land.

Coastal highlands are found around the plains. Rocky **cliffs** rise up from the ocean in the west.

bog

Cliffs of Moher

Size: more than 700 feet (213 meters) tall at its highest point

Famous For: large sea cliffs with beautiful views

Winters are mild in Ireland. Summers are cool.

Ireland has many rainy days. Some places may get over 100 inches (254 centimeters) of rain each year!

Different animals live in Ireland. Irish stoats hunt hares across the country. Puffins fly above the western coastline.

Atlantic puffins

Animals of Ireland

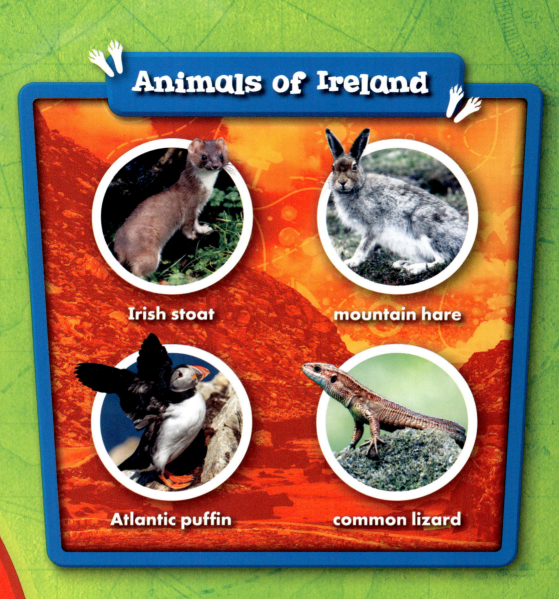

Irish stoat

mountain hare

Atlantic puffin

common lizard

Common lizards live by bogs. They are Ireland's only **reptile**!

Life in Ireland

The Irish mostly speak English. Some also speak Irish. Many are **Roman Catholics**.

Most people live in cities. But some live in the countryside.

Catholic church

The Irish love sharing stories. Many like **traditional** Irish music.

They also enjoy playing sports. **Gaelic football** and **hurling** are popular. Soccer is also a favorite.

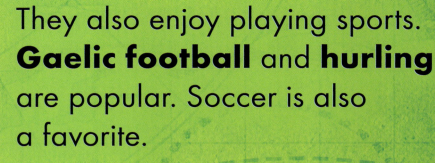

hurling

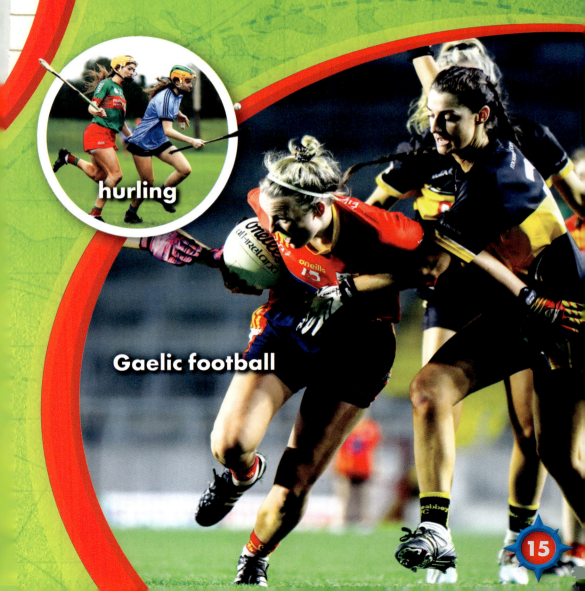

Gaelic football

Most Irish families make soda bread.
Potatoes are a **staple** food.
They are in meals like colcannon.

Irish Foods

soda bread

potatoes

colcannon

barmbrack

Barmbrack is a fruitcake.
It is eaten on Halloween!

Ireland's national holiday is Saint Patrick's Day. It is on March 17. People watch parades and wear green.

Saint Patrick's Day

May Day is in early May.
Families gather to welcome summer!

Ireland Facts

Size:
27,133 square miles
(70,273 square kilometers)

Population:
5,275,004 (2022)

National Holiday:
Saint Patrick's Day (March 17)

Main Languages:
English, Irish (Gaelic or Gaelige)

Capital City:
Dublin

Famous Face

Name: Niall Horan

Famous For: popular musician and former member of the band One Direction

Religions

- Church of Ireland: 3%
- other: 9%
- Roman Catholic: 78%
- none: 10%

Top Landmarks

Cliffs of Moher

Ring of Kerry

St. Patrick's Cathedral

21

Glossary

bogs—areas of wet ground found near bodies of water

cliffs—high, steep surfaces of rock, earth, or ice

Gaelic football—a team sport that is similar to soccer and rugby

hurling—an outdoor game played with a stick and ball, similar to field hockey and lacrosse

plains—large areas of flat land

reptile—a cold-blooded animal that has a backbone and lays eggs

Roman Catholics—people belonging or relating to the Christian church that is led by the pope

staple—a widely used food or other item

traditional—related to the customs, ideas, or beliefs handed down from one generation to the next

To Learn More

AT THE LIBRARY

Blevins, Wiley. *Ireland*. New York, N.Y.: Scholastic, 2018.

Dean, Jessica. *Ireland*. Minneapolis, Minn.: Pogo Books, 2019.

Reader, Jack. *The Story Behind St. Patrick's Day*. New York, N.Y.: PowerKids Press, 2020.

ON THE WEB

FACTSURFER

Factsurfer.com gives you a safe, fun way to find more information.

1. Go to www.factsurfer.com.

2. Enter "Ireland" into the search box and click 🔍.

3. Select your book cover to see a list of related content.

Index

animals, 10, 11
bogs, 6, 11
capital (see Dublin)
cities, 12
Cliffs of Moher, 7
Dublin, 4, 5
English, 12, 13
Europe, 4
food, 16, 17
Gaelic football, 15
Halloween, 17
hurling, 15
Ireland facts, 20–21
Irish, 12, 13
lakes, 6
map, 5

May Day, 19
music, 14
people, 12, 18
plains, 6
rain, 9
Roman Catholics, 12
Saint Patrick's Day, 18
say hello, 13
soccer, 15
summers, 8
winters, 8

The images in this book are reproduced through the courtesy of: Travel-Fr, cover; essevu, cover; Semmick Photo, p. 3; STUDIO MELANGE, pp. 4-5; Steve Allen, p. 6; Markus Moinka, pp. 6-7; Monicami, pp. 8-9; Jan Stria, p. 9; dit:Gert Hilbink, pp. 10-11; Bogdan P, p. 11 (Irish stoat); Sandra Standbridge, p. 11 (mountain hare); Piotr Poznan, p. 11 (Atlantic puffin); Marek R. Swadzba, p. 11 (common lizard); JeniFoto, 12; Lisa5201, pp. 12-13; Jon Chica, pp. 14-15; D. Ribeiro, pp. 15, (main, inset); Melica, p. 16 (soda bread); Tayvay, p. 16 (potatoes); Slawomir Fajer, p. 16 (colcannon); Happy Foods Tube, p. 16 (barmbrack); Image Source, p. 17; Peter Cavanage/ Alamy, pp. 18-19; titoOnz, p. 20 (flag); Featureflash Photo Agency, p. 20 (Niall Horan); AJ Abell, p. 21 (Cliffs of Moher); Dawid K Photography, p. 21 (Ring of Kerry); Nabil Imran, p. 21 (St. Patrick's Cathedral); Algirdas Gelazious, pp. 22-23.

24